THE PERSON BEHIND THE BRAND

MICHAEL JORDAN

WRITTEN BY ANNETTE WHIPPLE

ILLUSTRATED BY GARY BOLLER

TABLE OF CONTENTS

A Starfish Book

SEAHORSE PUBLISHING

Teaching Tips for Caregivers:

As a caregiver, you can help your child succeed in school by giving them a strong foundation in language and literacy skills and a desire to learn to read.

This book helps children grow by letting them practice reading skills.

Reading for pleasure and interest will help your child develop reading skills and will give your child the opportunity to practice these skills in meaningful ways.

- Encourage your child to read on their own at home.
- Encourage your child to practice reading aloud.
- Encourage activities that require reading.
- Establish a reading time.
- Talk with your child.
- Give your child writing materials.

Teaching Tips for Teachers:

Research shows that one of the best ways for students to learn a new topic is to read about it.

Before Reading

- Read the "Words to Know" and discuss the meaning of each word.
- Read the back cover to see what the book is about.

During Reading

- When a student gets to a word that is unknown, ask them to look at the rest of the sentence to find clues to help with the meaning of the unknown word.
- Ask the student to write down any pages of the book that were confusing to them.

After Reading

- Discuss the main idea of the book.
- Ask students to give one detail that they learned from the book by showing a text-dependent answer from the book.

MICHAEL JORDAN—AIR JORDAN

Michael Jordan made Nike sneakers famous.

It took a lot of hard work.

Michael was born in 1963.

He grew up in Wilmington, North Carolina.

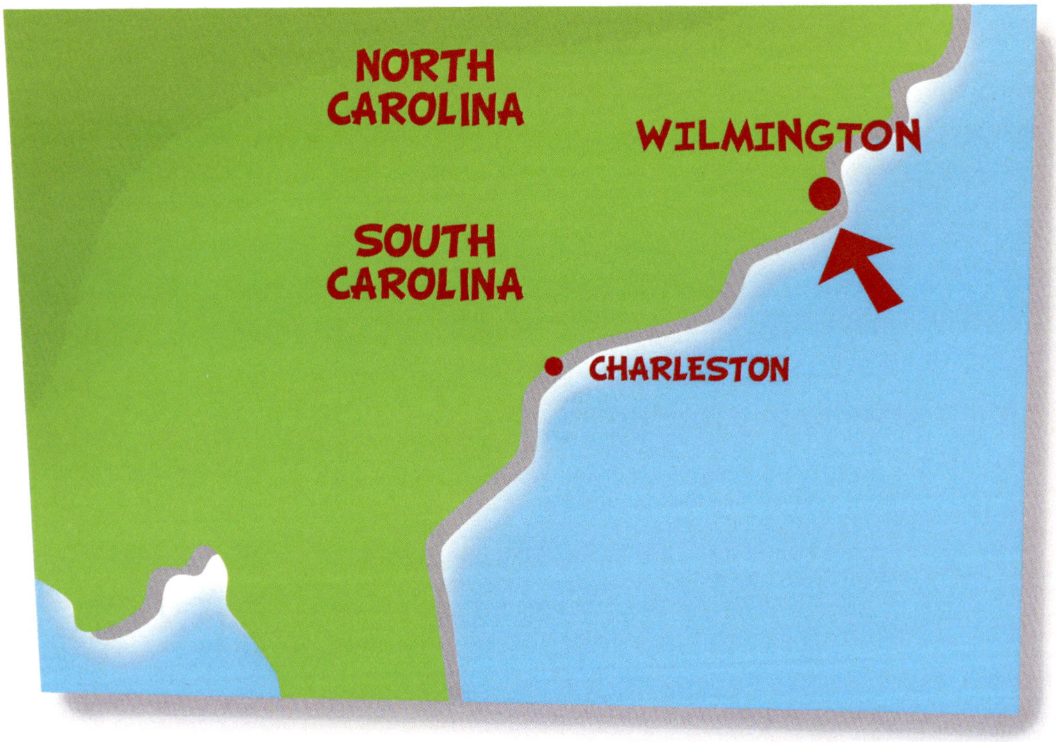

Michael loved playing basketball with his brother.

Their dad built a basketball court in the backyard.

Michael tried out for his high school **varsity** basketball team.

He only made the junior varsity team.

Michael kept working hard.

The next year, he made the varsity team.

Michael played basketball in college.

People noticed all the points he scored.

He became a basketball **star**.

BULLS
23
BOING!
SWOOP!!
BULLS
23

Michael played for the Chicago Bulls.

He jumped to make baskets.

It looked like he was flying through the air.

Shoe **companies** wanted famous **athletes** to wear their shoes.

Michael's parents helped him choose the best deal.

Nike paid Michael to wear their sneakers.

People at Nike showed Michael some red and black sneakers.

Michael had ideas to make them even better.

Nike listened to him and made changes.

Michael and Nike made a deal.

They called Michael's sneakers Air Jordans.

People loved to wear Air Jordans.

Michael became successful in the shoe **business**.

He also kept playing basketball.

He won many awards.

Michael was a **champion**.

Many people think he is the best basketball player of all time.

MICHAEL JORDAN

in 2006

Air Jordan sneakers are still popular today.

WORDS TO KNOW

athletes (ATH-leets): people who are very good at playing a sport

business (BIZ-nis): activity related to selling things

champion (CHAM-pee-uhn): someone who has won many competitions

companies (KUHM-puh-neez): organizations that make and sell products or services

star (stahr): a person who is outstanding at doing an activity

varsity (VAHR-suh-tee): the team that has the best players at a school

INDEX

COMPREHENSION QUESTIONS

1. Michael Jordan is famous for playing ________ .
   a. basketball
   b. soccer
   c. hockey

2. Michael's ________ helped him decide to work with Nike.
   a. coaches
   b. parents
   c. teammates

3. Michael and Nike created sneakers called ________ .
   a. Air Jumpers
   b. Sky Jordans
   c. Air Jordans

4. True or false: Michael was part of every team he tried out for.

5. True or false: Michael Jordan played for the Chicago Bulls.

Answers:
1. a, 2. b, 3. c, 4. False, 5. True

ABOUT THE AUTHOR

Annette Whipple celebrates curiosity through her books. She wrote *The Laura Ingalls Wilder Companion*, *Whooo Knew? The Truth About Owls*, and *Quirky Critter Devotions*. She lives with her family in Pennsylvania where she appreciates the natural beauty around her. Get to know Annette at www.AnnetteWhipple.com.

ABOUT THE ILLUSTRATOR

Gary Boller lives in the glorious countryside in Hampshire, UK, with his wife and two children, one Chihuahua, and four cats. He always doodled as a kid, even on his parents' walls, and loved the comics of the day. Gary also loves music and has played double bass in bands. He has toured all over Europe many times and the USA twice. He's currently learning fiddle, much to the annoyance of his pets.

Written by: Annette Whipple
Illustrated by: Gary Boller
Designed by: Under the Oaks
Editor: Kim Thompson
Production manager:
Candice Campbell

Library of Congress PCN Data
Michael Jordan / Annette Whipple
The Person Behind the Brand
ISBN 979-8-8945-9118-6 (hard cover)
ISBN 979-8-8945-9123-0 (paperback)
ISBN 979-8-8945-9133-9 (EPUB)
ISBN 979-8-8945-9128-5 (eBook)
Library of Congress Control Number: 2024946245

Printed in the U.S.A./CP112025

Seahorse Publishing Company
www.seahorsepub.com

Published in the United States
Seahorse Publishing
PO Box 771325
Coral Springs, FL 33077

SEAHORSE PUBLISHING